This is a tale of
Two Heads

In the same series
Two Wheels Two Heads

The One and Only
TWO HEADS

Janet and Allan Ahlberg

Collins Glasgow and London

First published 1979
Published by William Collins Sons and Company Limited Glasgow and London

Printed in Great Britain
ISBN 0 00 138034 6

One morning Two Heads sits up in bed.
He is beside himself.
Half of him has a secret and will not tell the other half.

Two Heads goes to the bathroom.
He washes his faces and cleans
his teeths.
But he does not tell himself
the secret.

Two Heads gets dressed.
He comes downstairs and eats
his breakfasts.
But still he does not tell
himself the secret.

Two Heads gets grumpy. He says he will fall out with himself if this goes on.

So at last the secret is revealed.
It is Two Heads' birthday!

Two Heads decides to have a party.

He decorates the room with paper chains and balloons.

He makes a cake and a jelly.

He makes some sandwiches,

two trifles and a jug of lemonade.

He makes a mess.

Oops!

The party begins.
First there are the games.
Two Heads plays ‘Spin the Plate’
and ‘Blindman’s Buff’.

He wins the quiz.
He comes first and second in
the 'Ugly Mugs' contest.

Happy birthday fellas!

Then there is a knock at the door and his friend Four Arms comes in.
Four Arms has a present for him.

Two Heads unwraps it

and unwraps it

and unwraps it.

What have we here?
It is a woolly jumper – just
what Two Heads needs.

Two Heads and Four Arms sit down to the birthday feast.

Pass the pop,
old pal!
Tuck in,
old chum!

They eat the jelly and the cake.
They eat the trifles and the
sandwiches.

They drink the lemonade.
They tell each other jokes.

wobble
wobble

After the birthday feast there is the birthday washing-up.

plonk
plonk

In the evening Four Arms plays the piano.
He does a bit of juggling too.

Now it is getting late.
Four Arms puts on his hat and scarf.

He puts on two pairs of gloves and goes home.

Two Heads goes to bed.
He puts the light out.
Then he puts it on again.
Half of him wants a glass
of water.

Two Heads says 'Goodnight' to himself.
In a little while he dreams sweet dreams . . .

. . . both of him.

THE END